This book belongs to

_____

_____

_____

Beginner-level handwriting book that will help kids to learn and improve their writing in an easy way. This book will develop the confidence of the kids to improve their writing ability.

Part 1: Learning the Alphabet with tracing letters a-z & A-Z

Part 2: Writing Numbers & Number Words 1 - 100

Part 3: Learning Sight Words

Part 4: Learning & Writing the Fruit's name

Part 5: Learning Simple Sentences

Let's do it

UPPERCASE HANDWRITING
PRACTICE

A B C D E F G

H I J K L M N

O P Q R S T

U V W X Y Z

Name: _____

LOWERCASE HANDWRITING PRACTICE

a b c d e f g

h i j k l m n o

p q r s t u v

w x y z

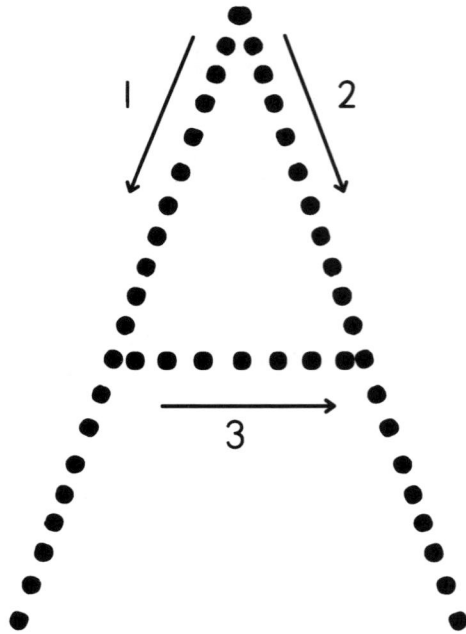
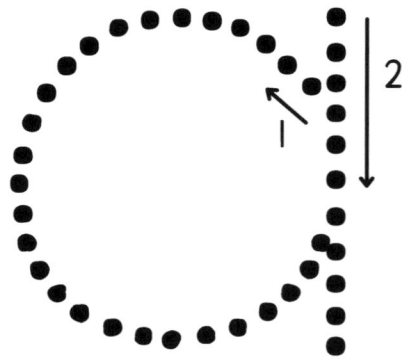

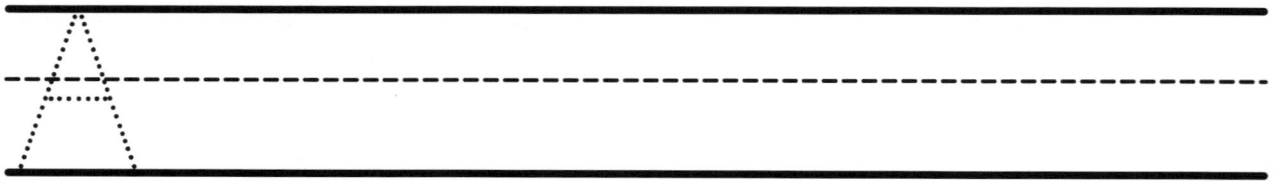

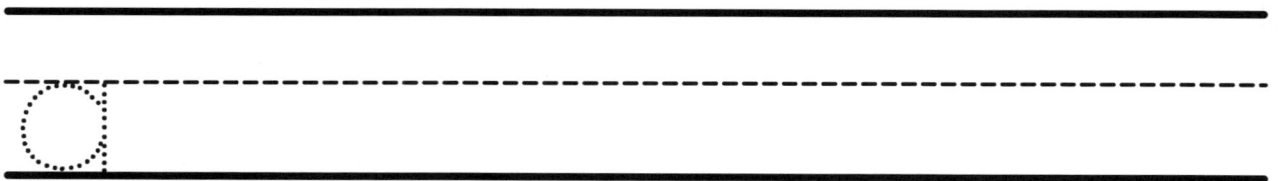

A

a

A

a

AaAaAaAaAaAa

Name

B for Ball

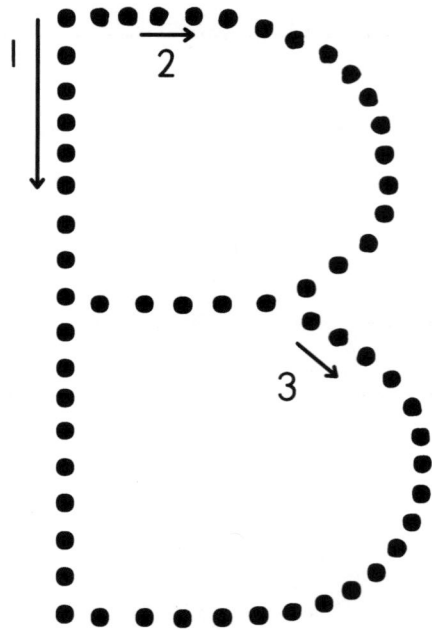
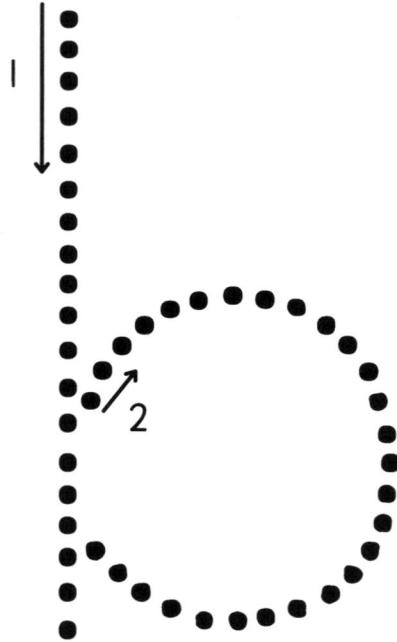

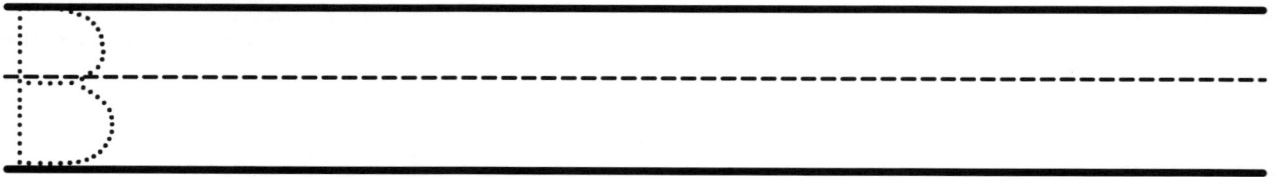

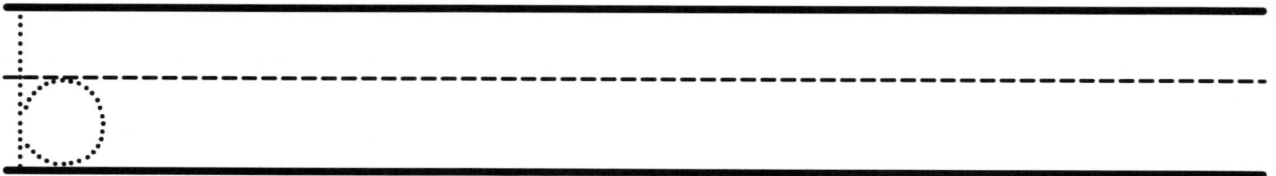

B

b

B

b

BbBbBbBb

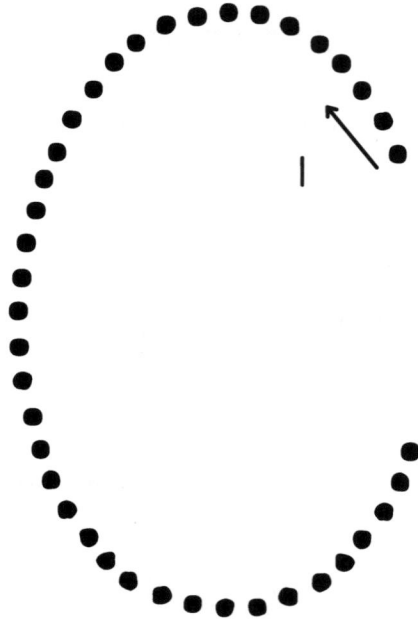
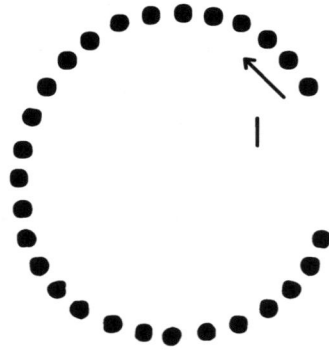

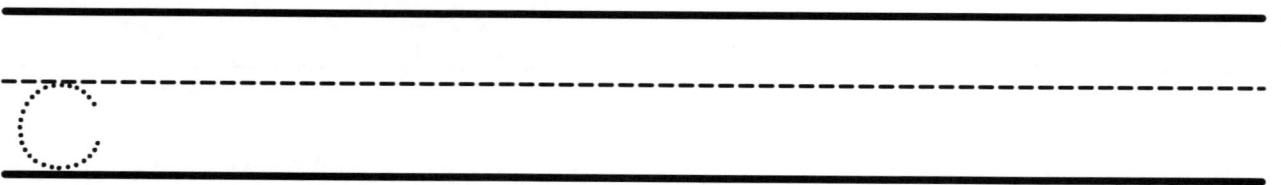

C

C

C

C

C c C c C c C c C c

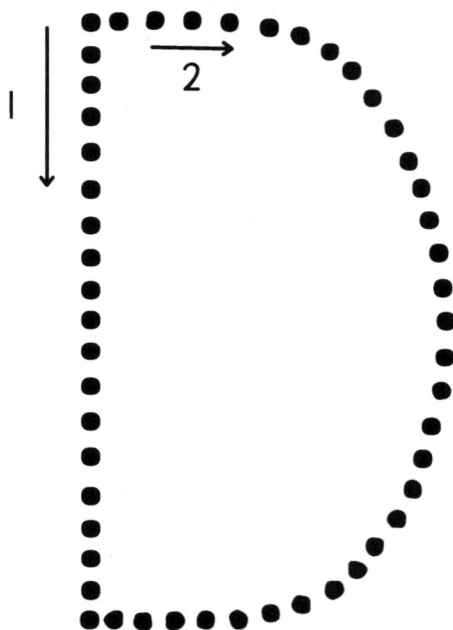
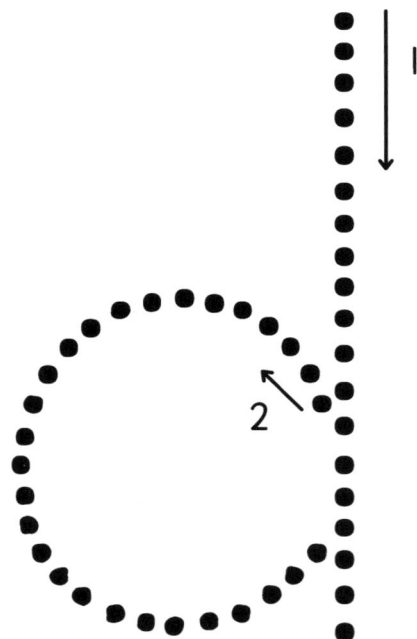

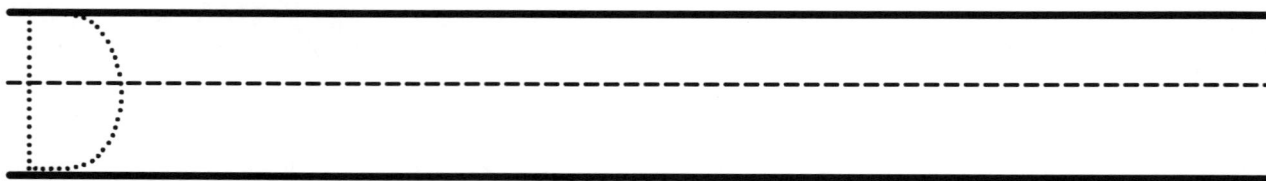

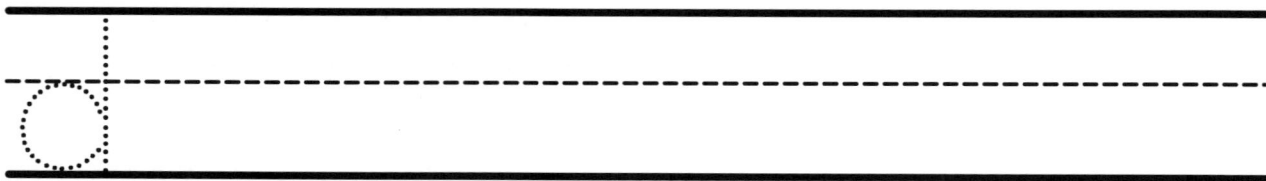

D

d

D

d

D d D d D d D d

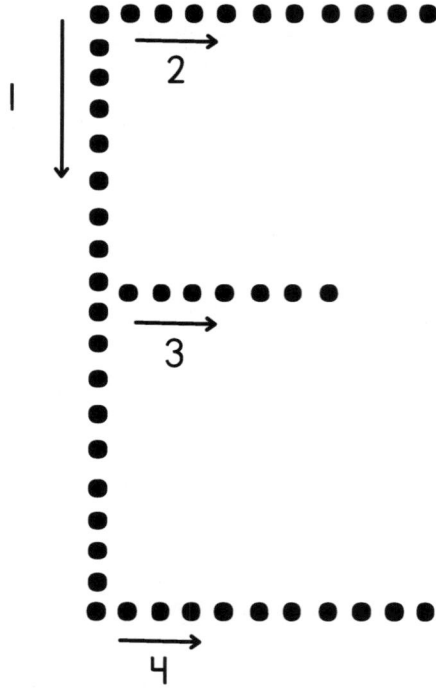

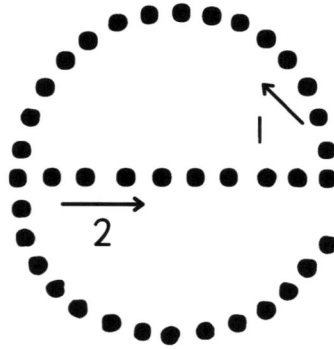

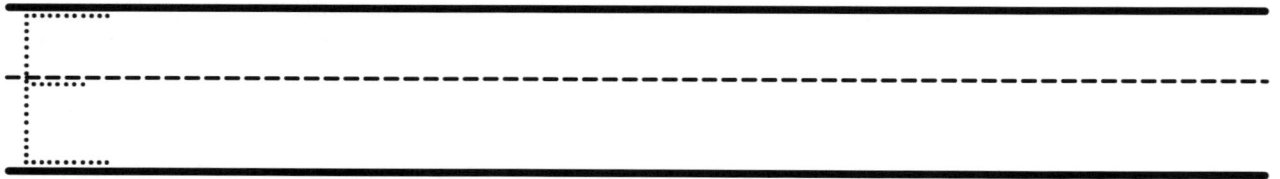

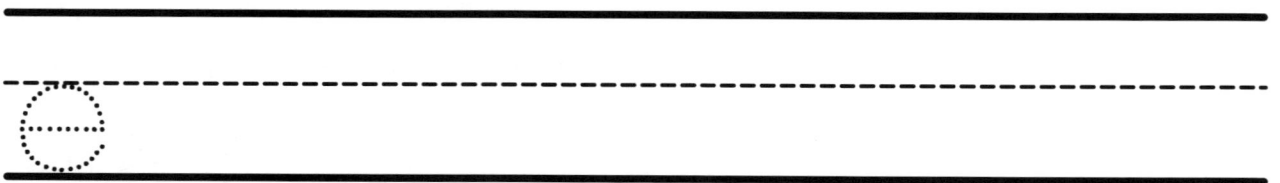

E

e

E

e

E e E e E e E e

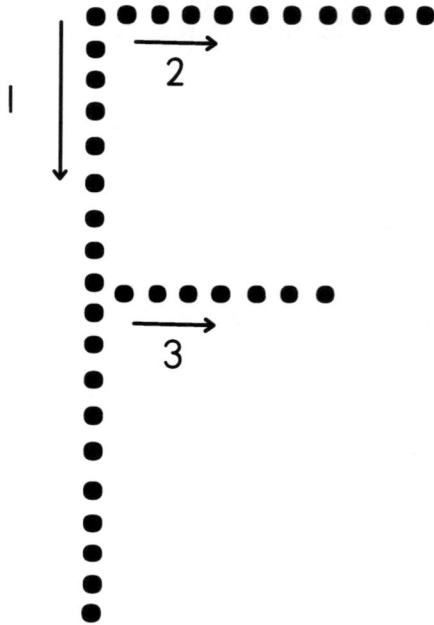
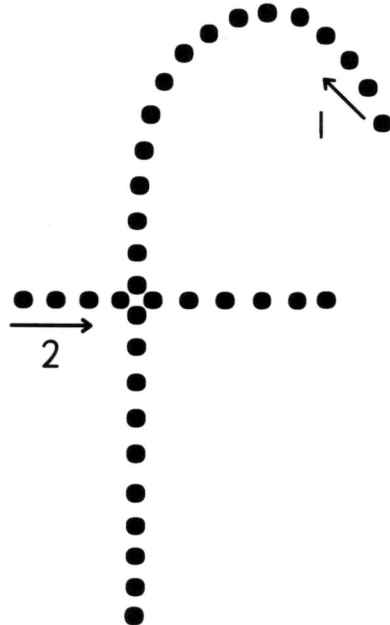

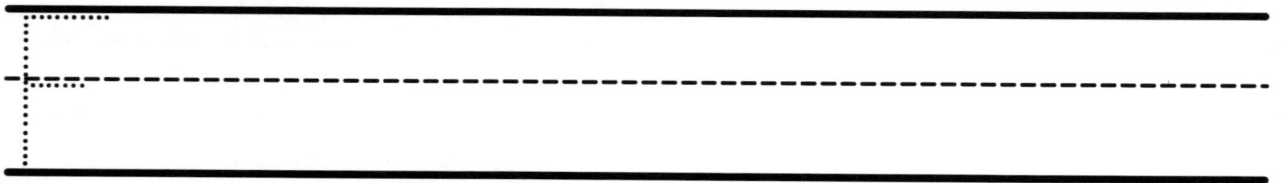

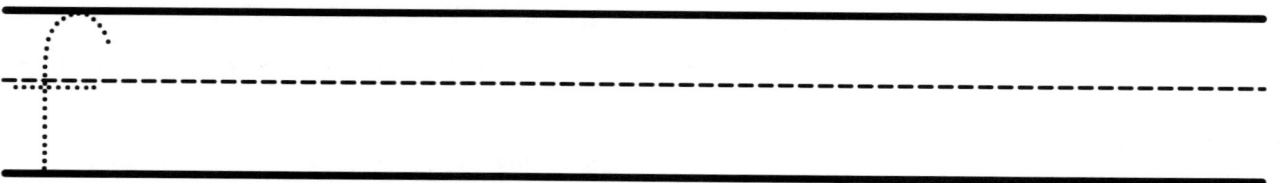

f f f f f f f

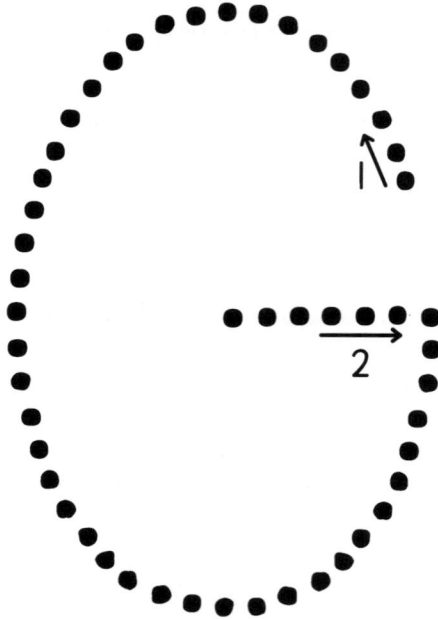

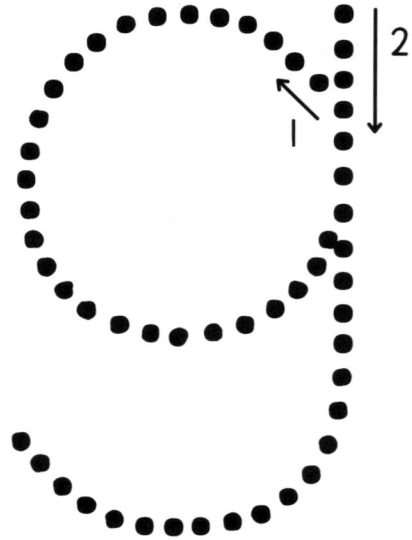

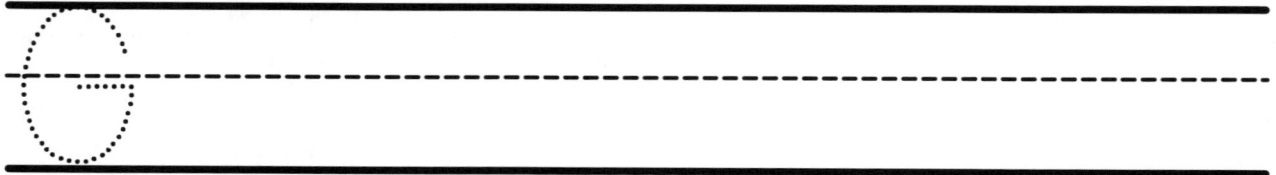

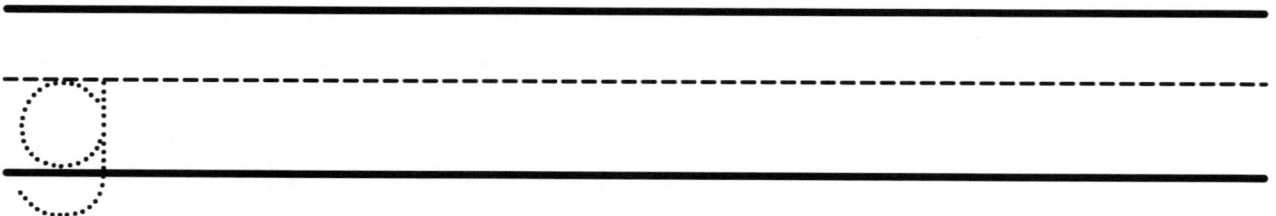

Gg Gg Gg Gg Gg Gg Gg Gg

H for House

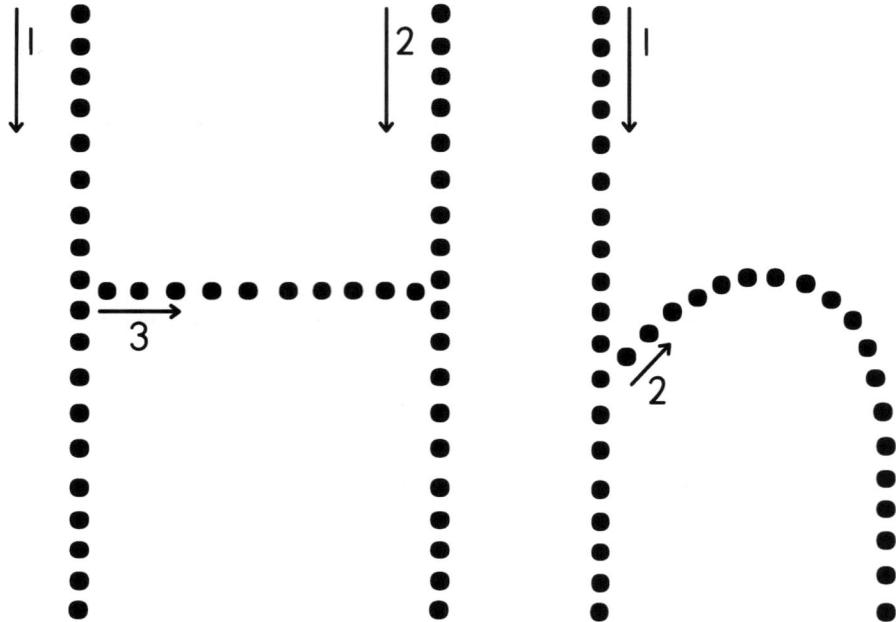

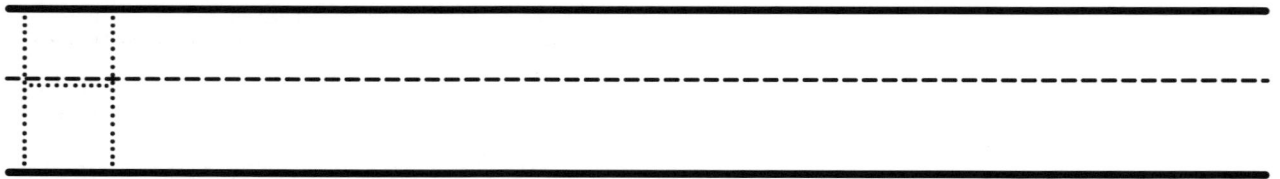

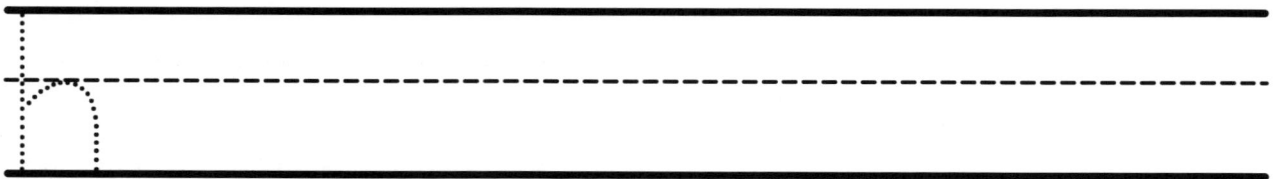

H

h

H

h

Hh h h h h h h h

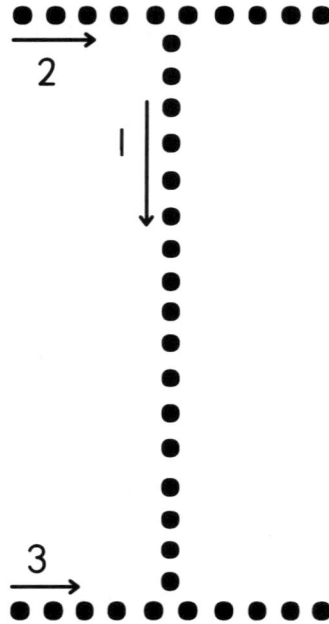
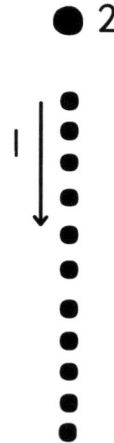

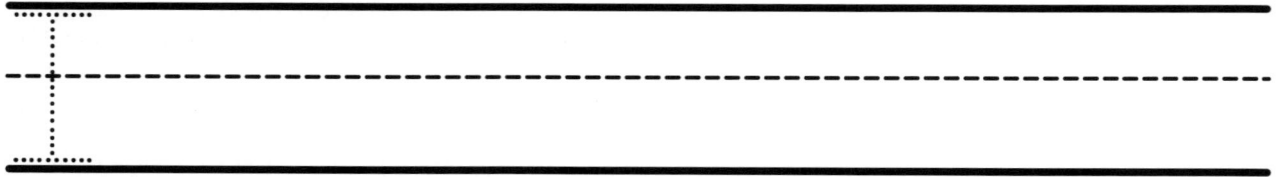

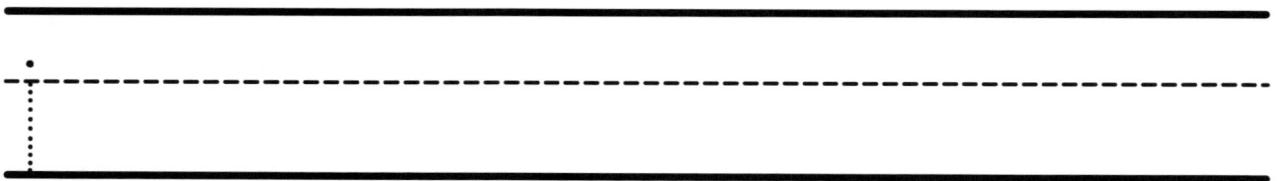

I
I
I
i
I I I I I I I I I I

J for Juice

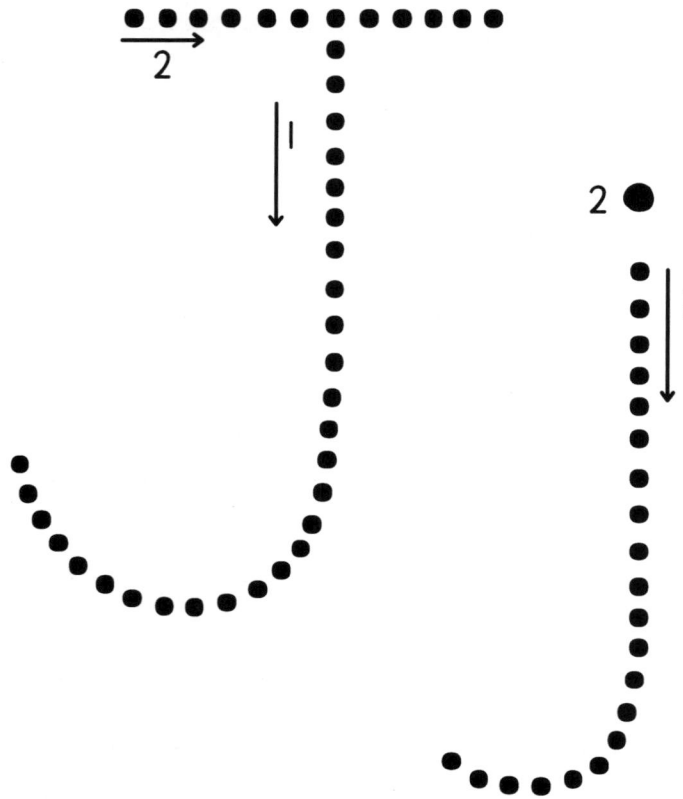

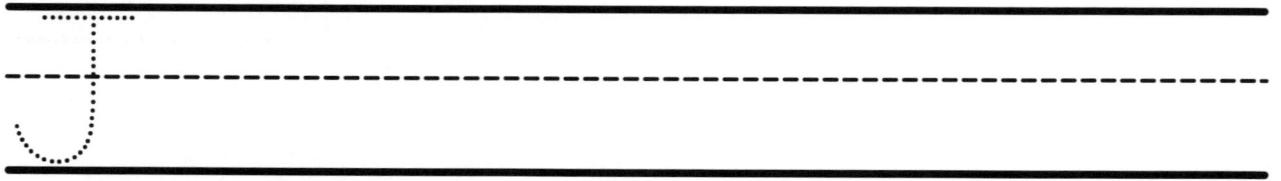

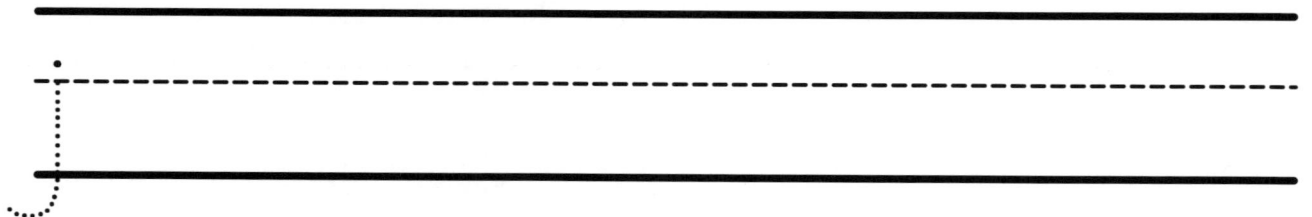

J

j

J

j

J j J j J j J j J j

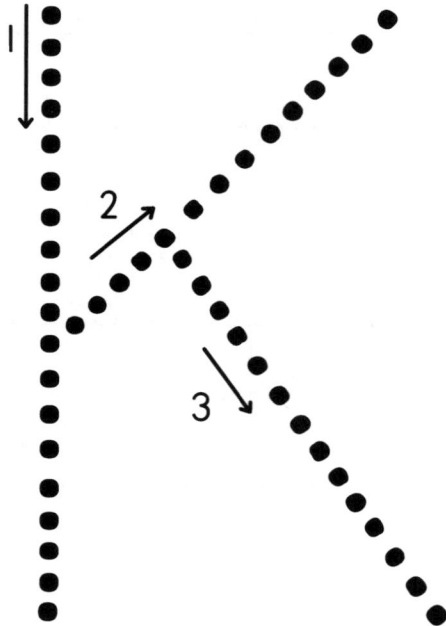
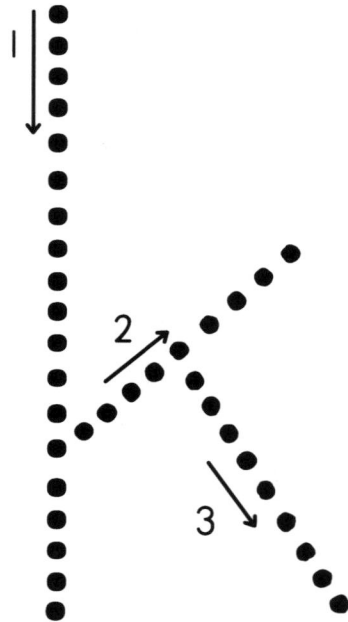

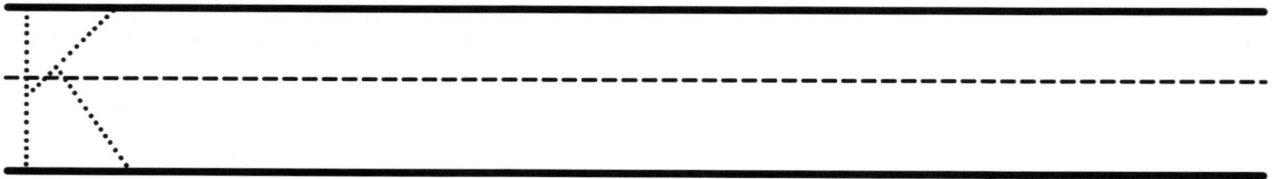

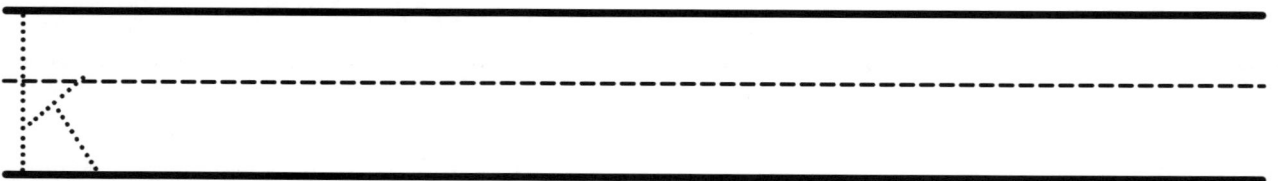

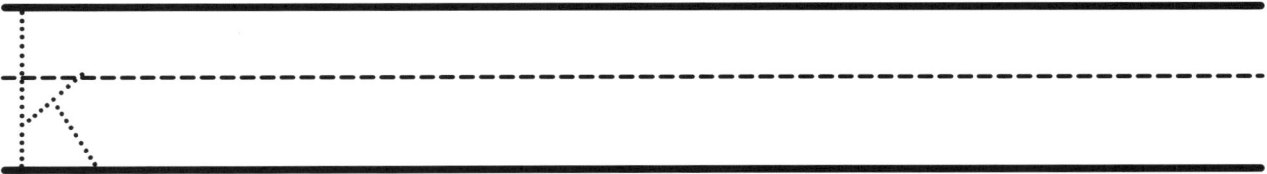

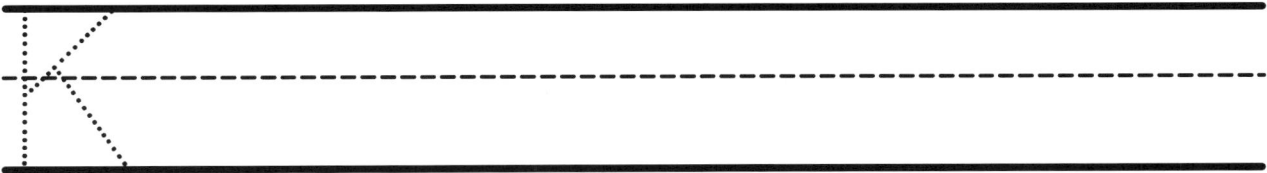

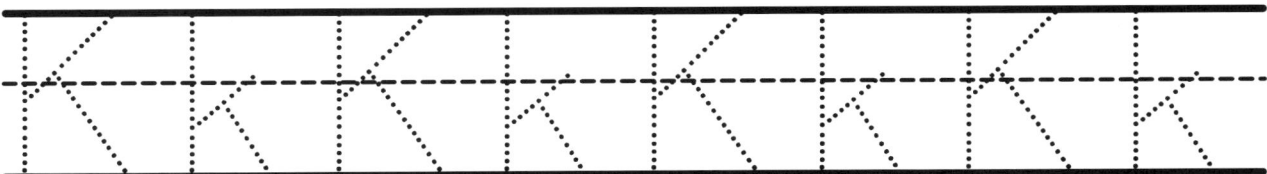

Name

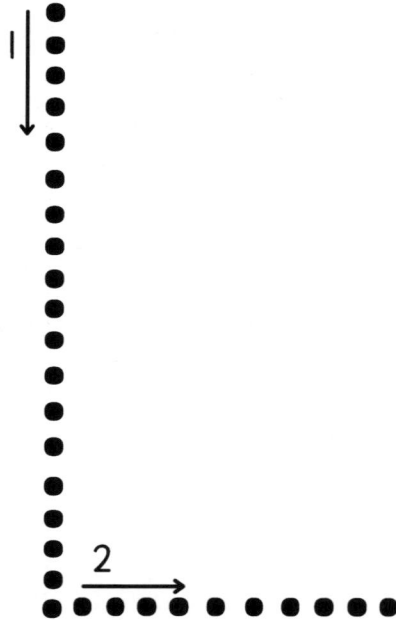

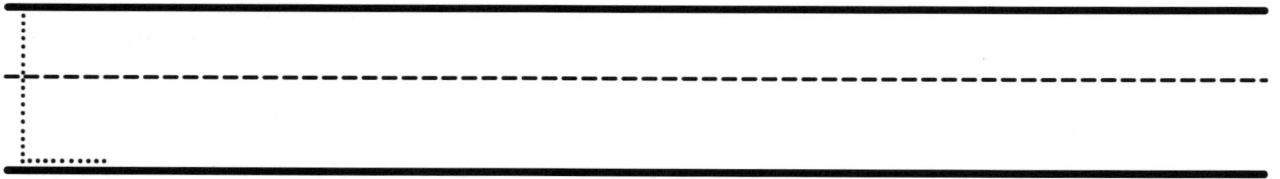

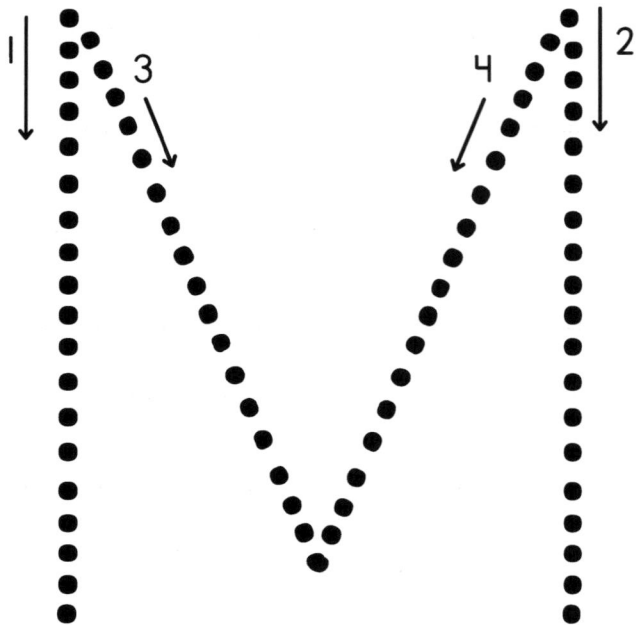
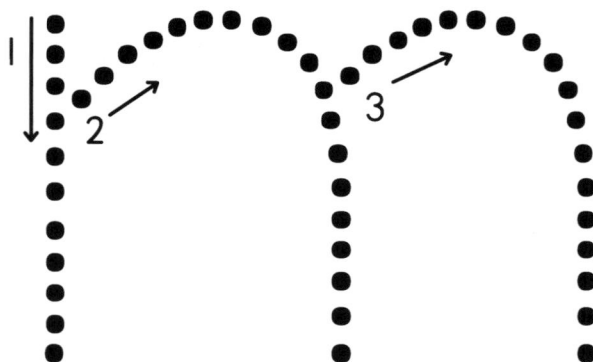

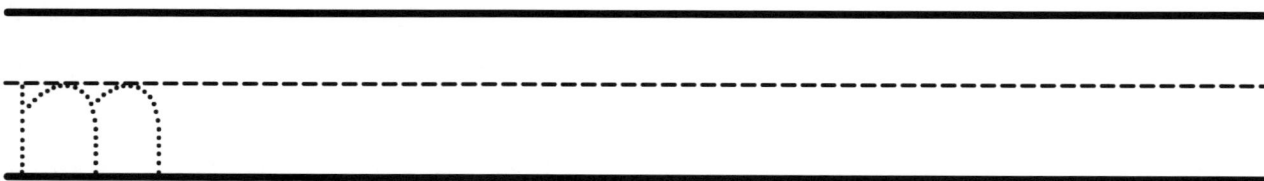

M

m

M

m

MmMmMmMmMmM

Name

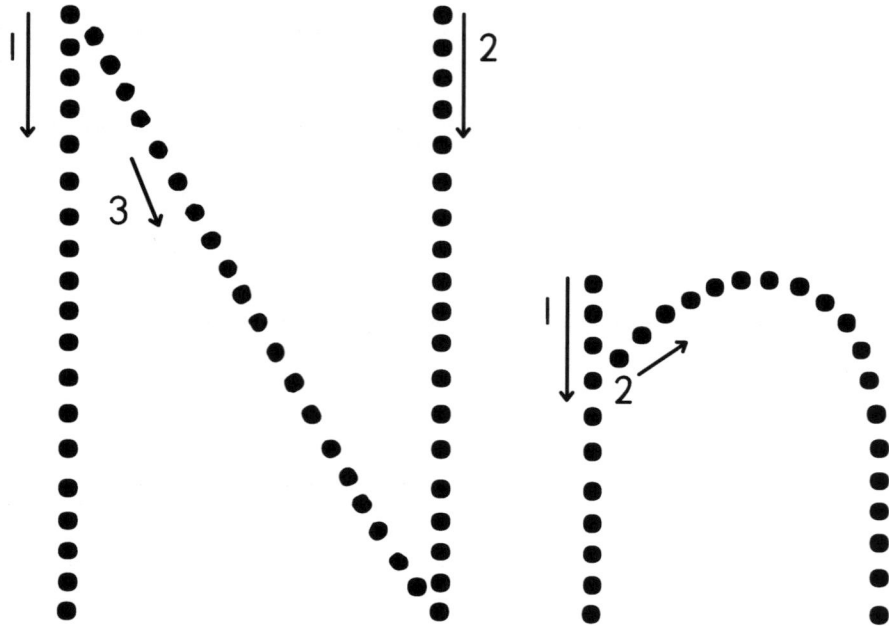

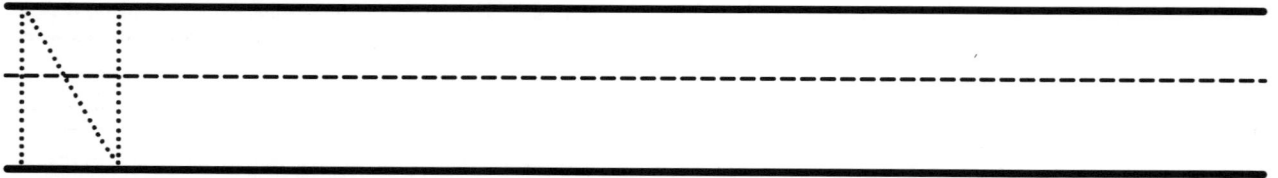

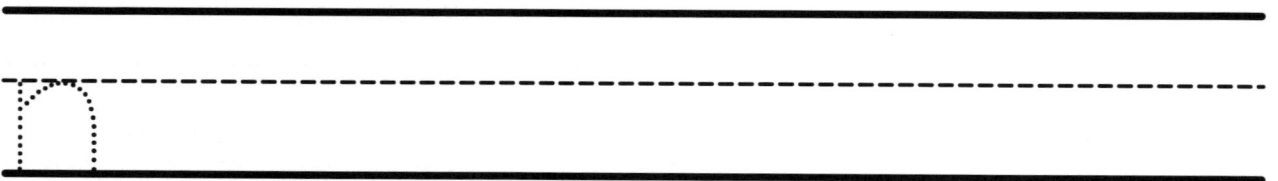

N

n

N

n

NnNnNnNnNnNn

Name

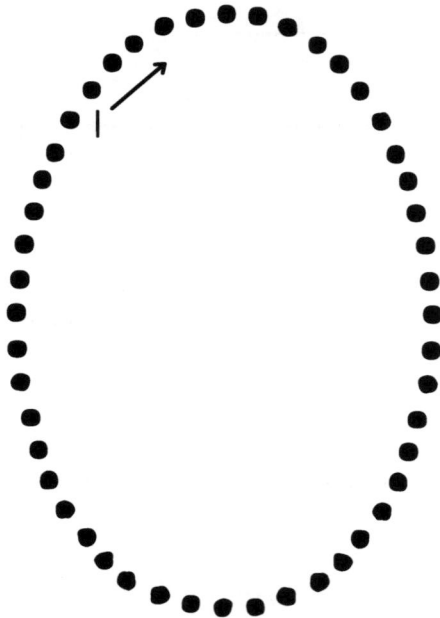

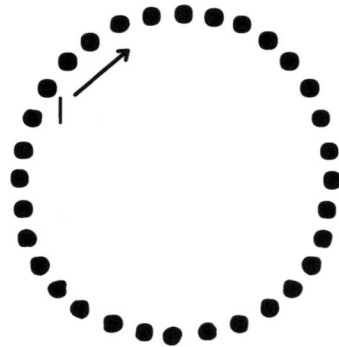

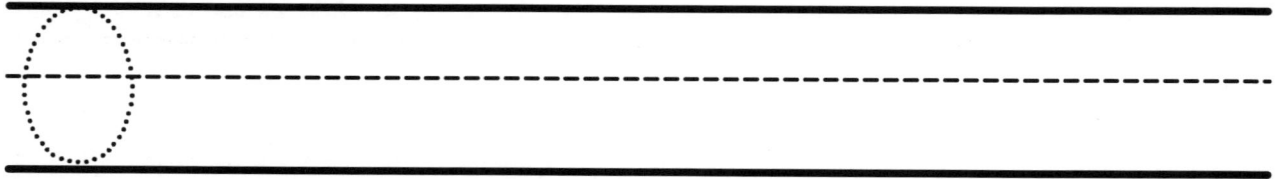

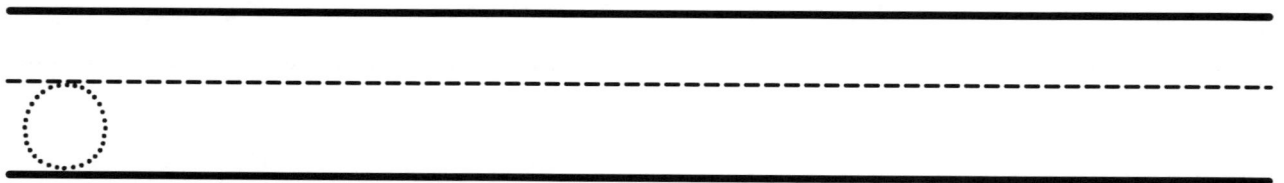

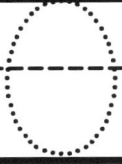

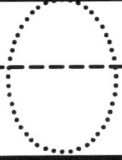

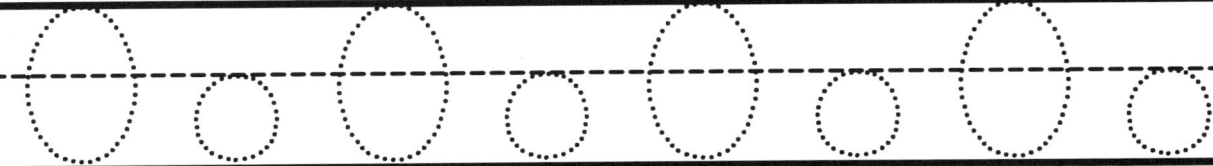

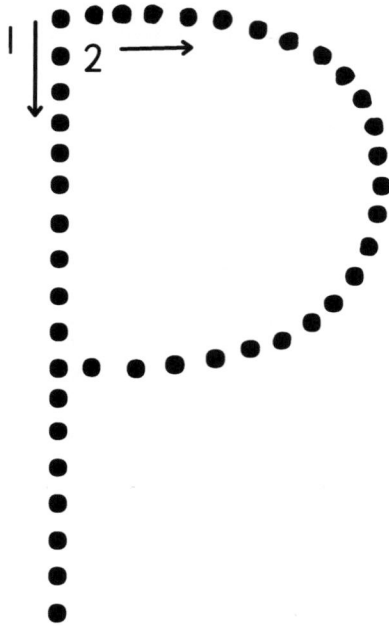

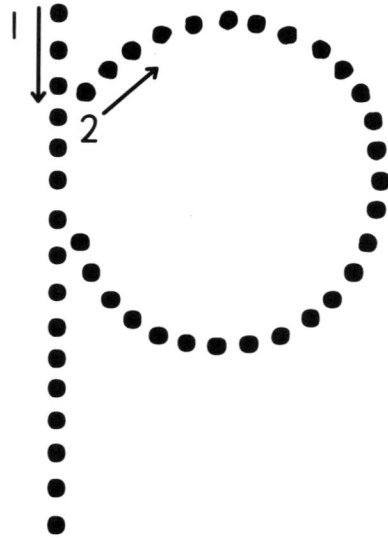

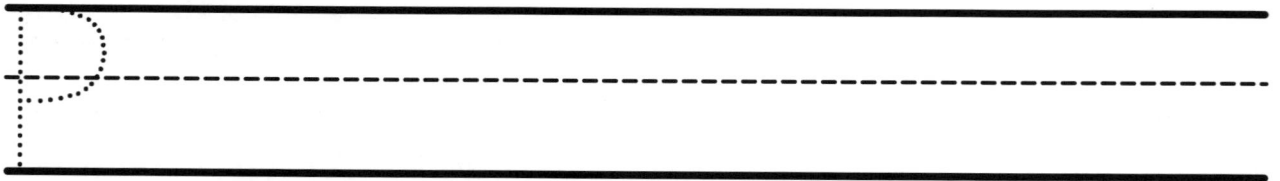

P

p

P

p

P p P p P p P p P p P p

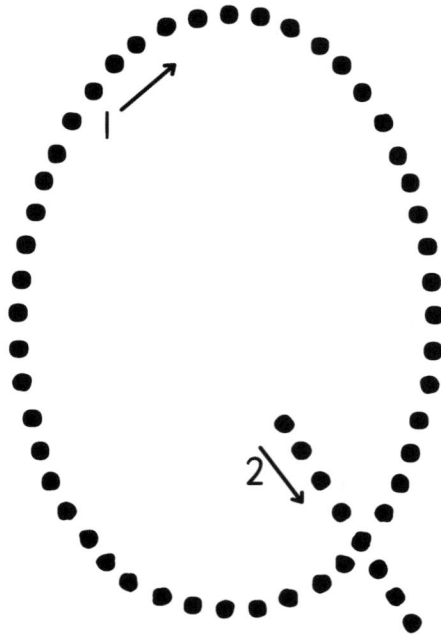

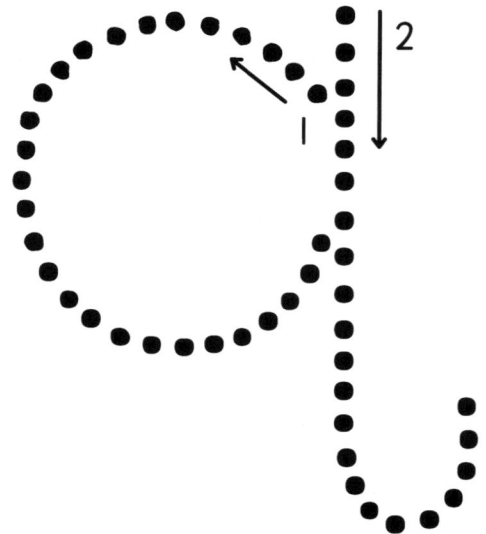

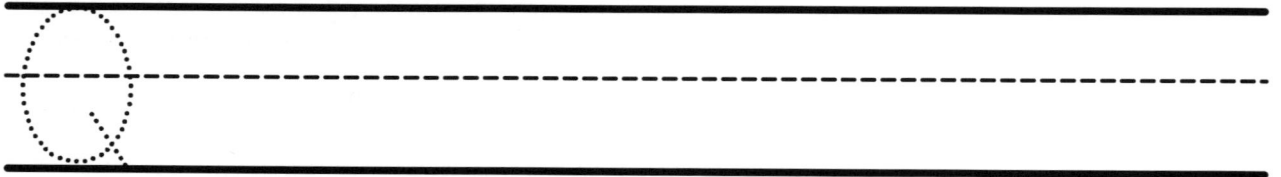

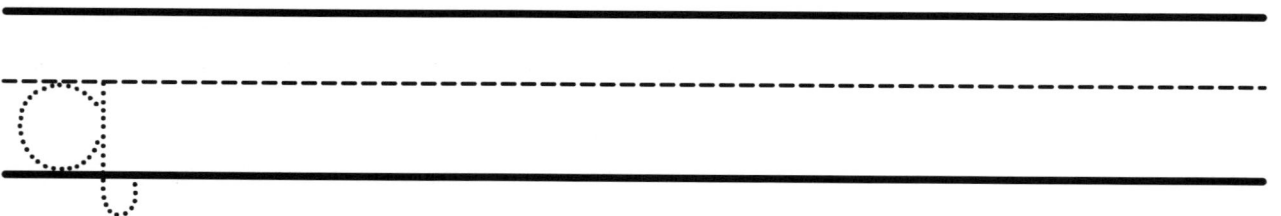

Q q Q q Q q Q q

Name

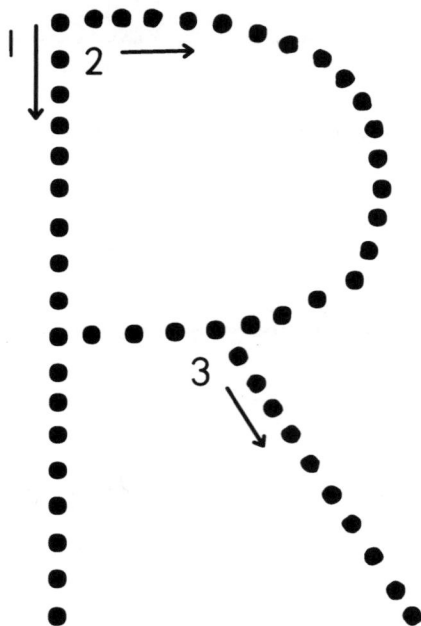

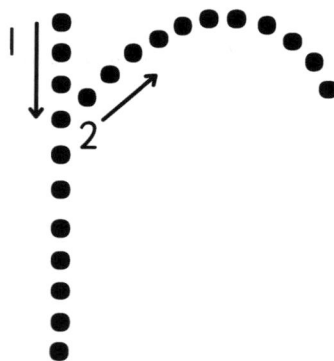

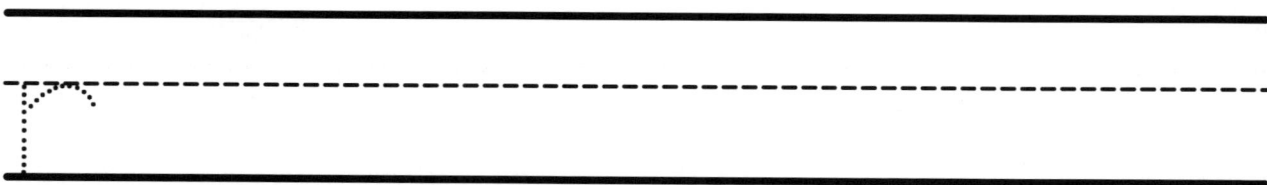

R

r

R

r

RrRrRrRr

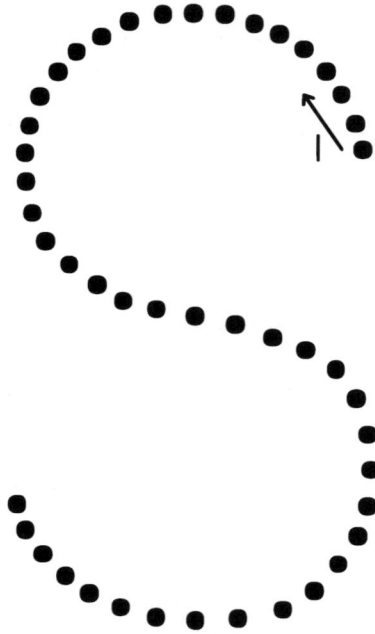

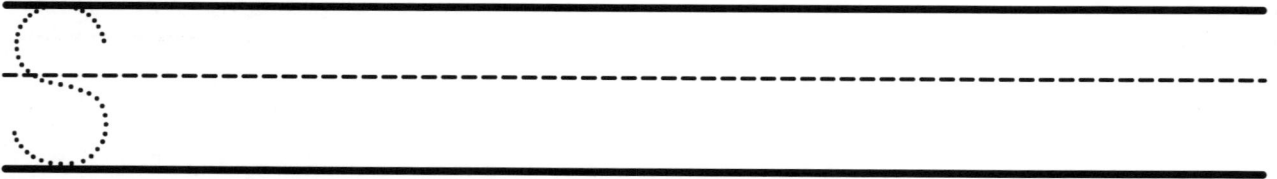

S

S

S

S

S S S S S S S S

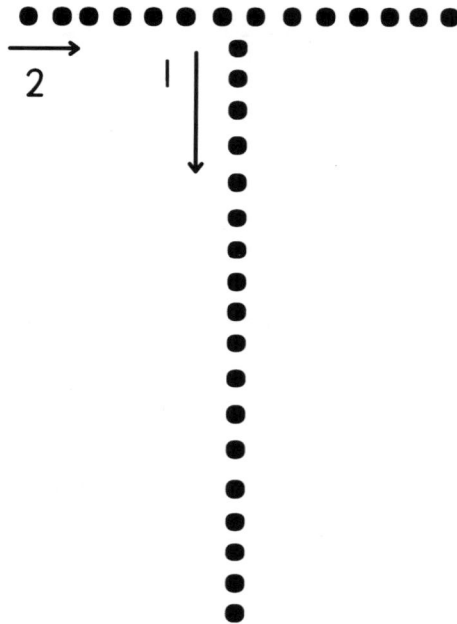

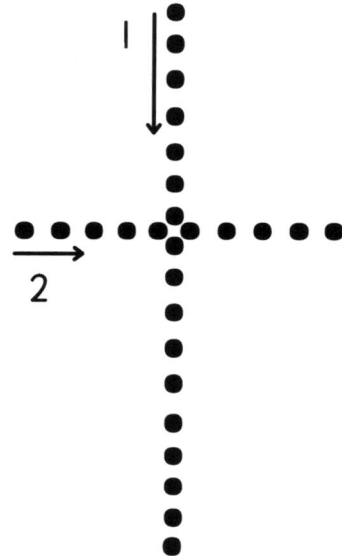

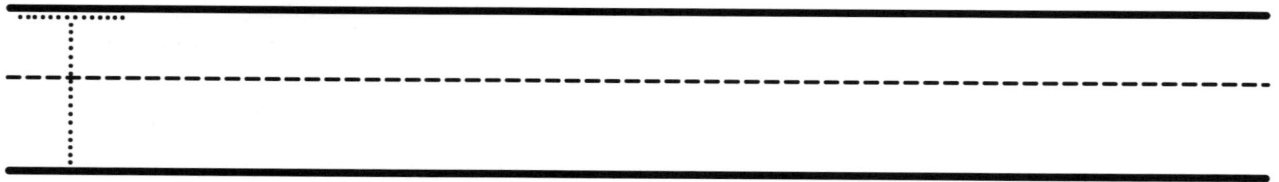

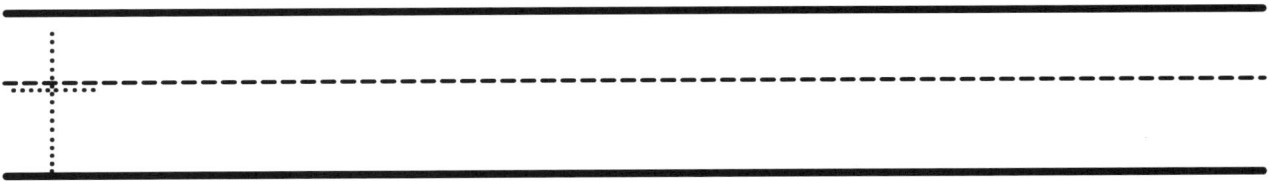

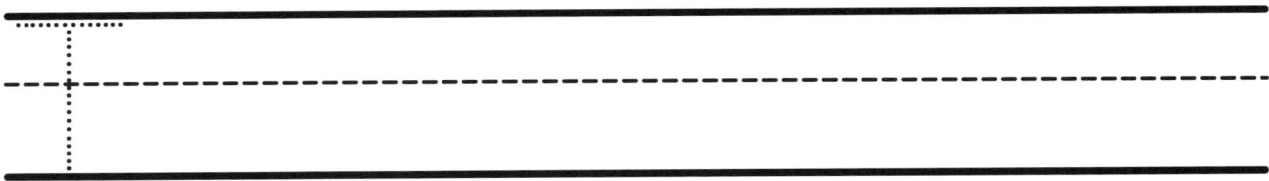

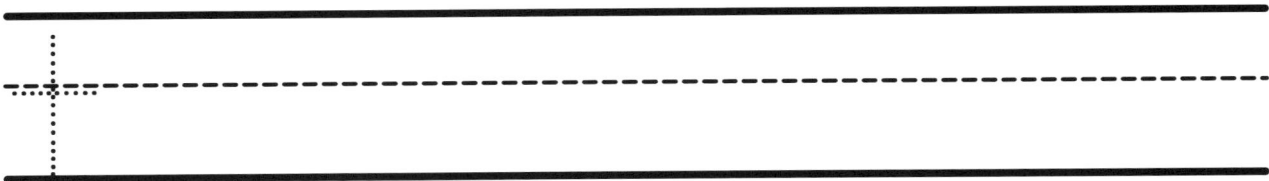

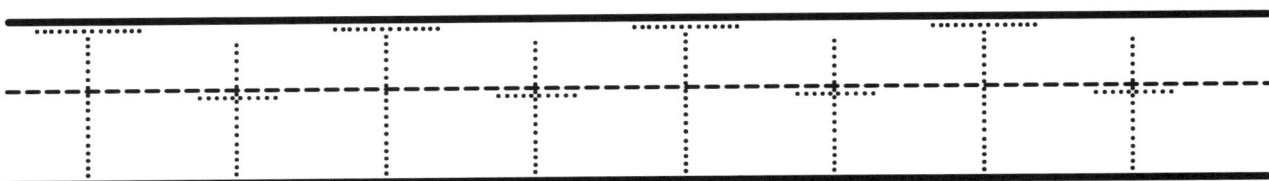

Name

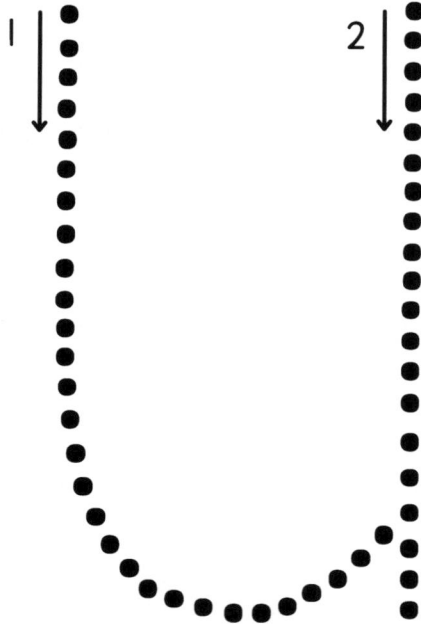

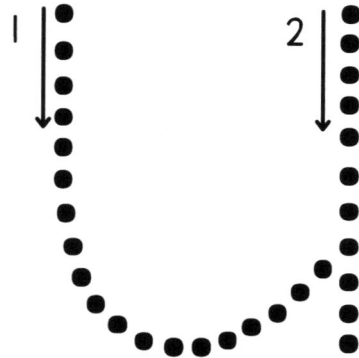

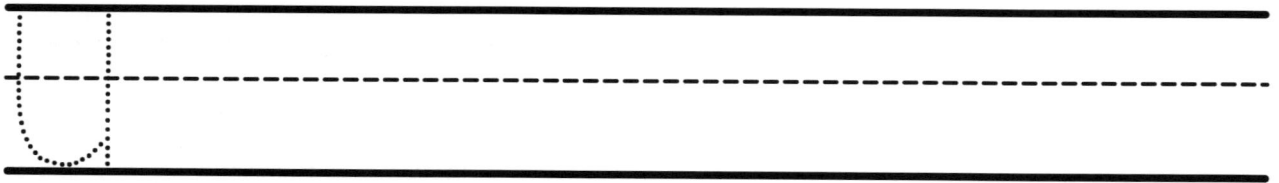

U U U U U U U U U

V for Vegetables

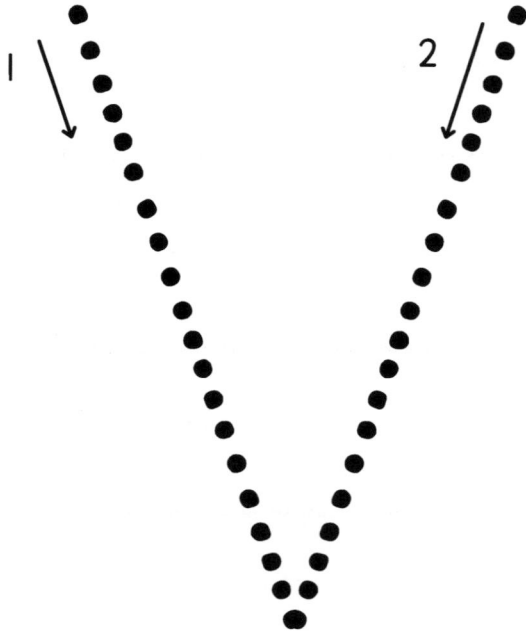

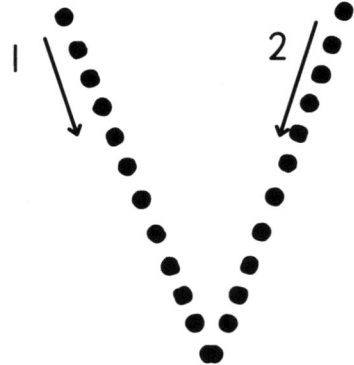

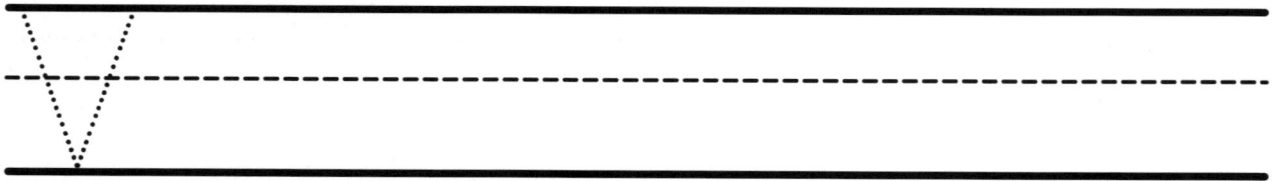

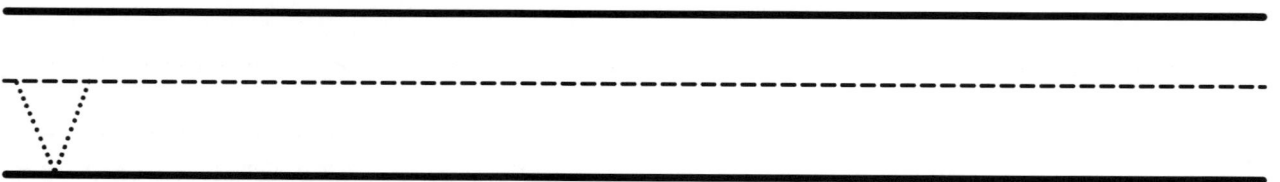

1

2

1

2

V

V

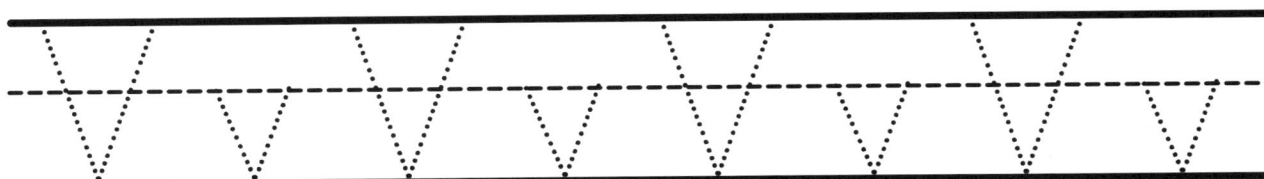

Name

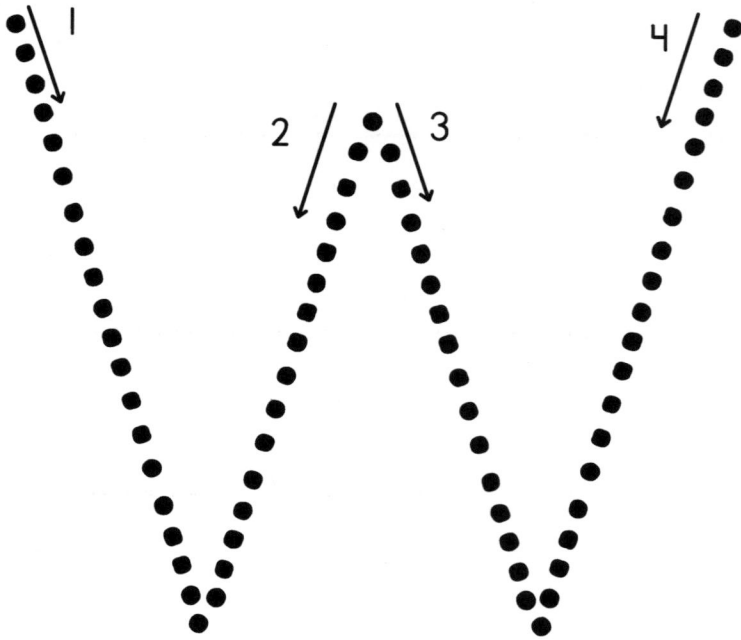
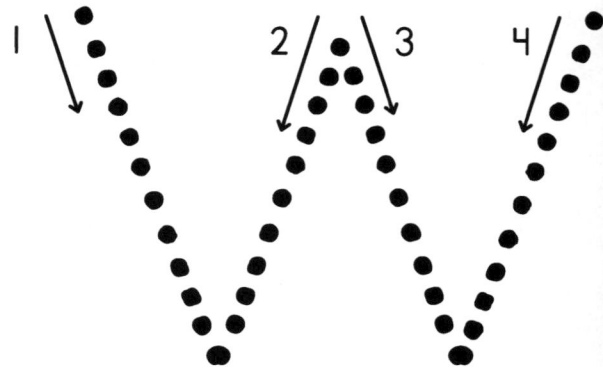

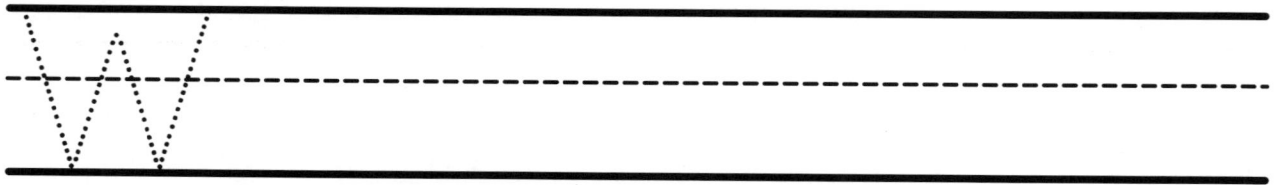

W w W w W W W w W w W w W w

X for Xylophone

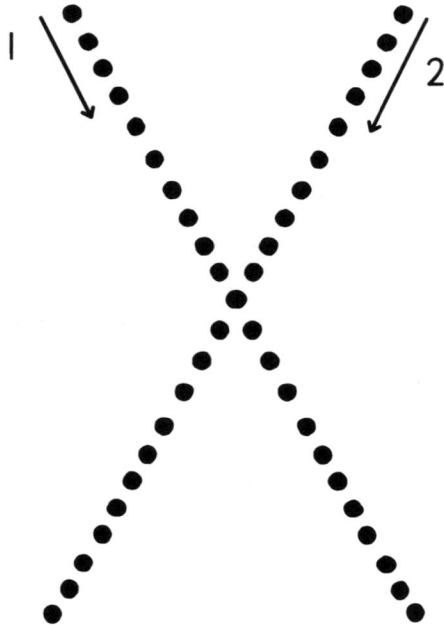

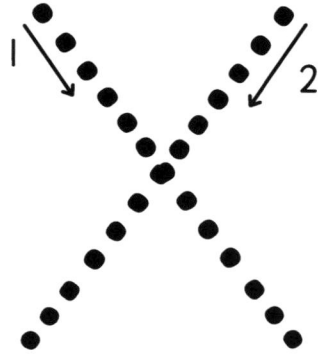

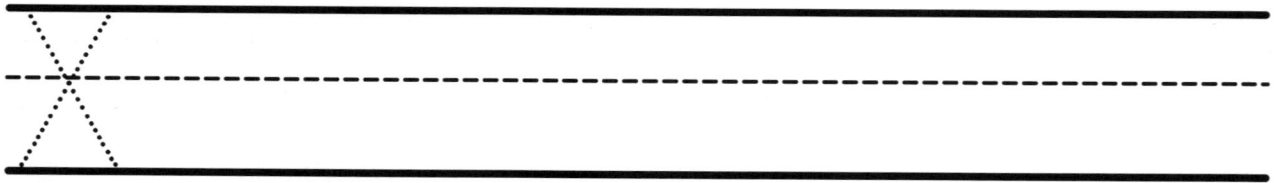

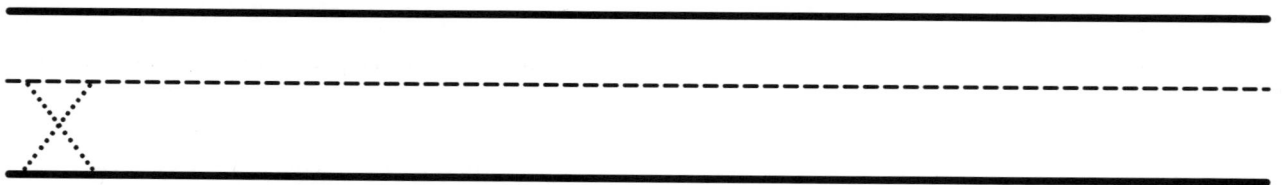

X

x

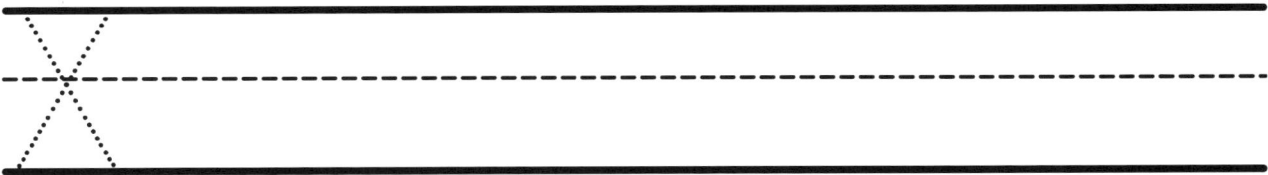

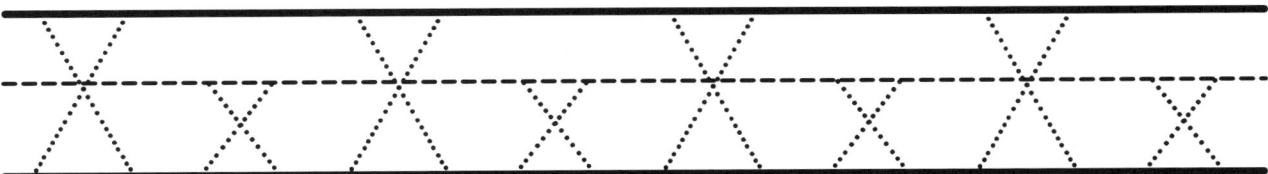

Name

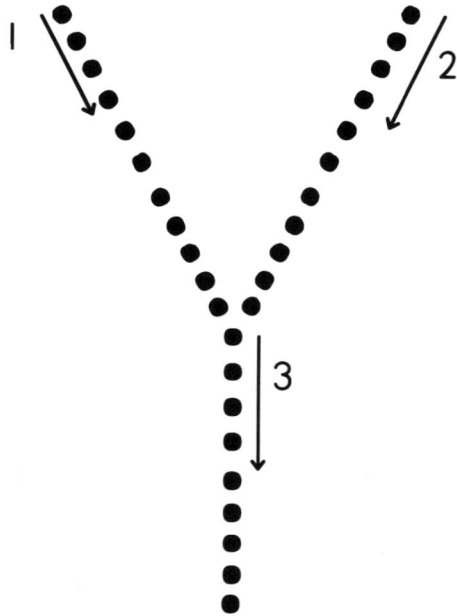

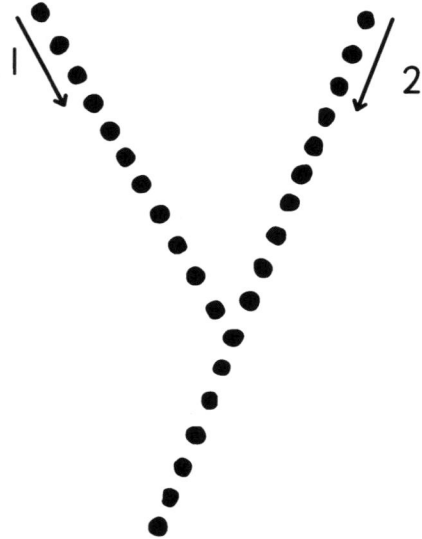

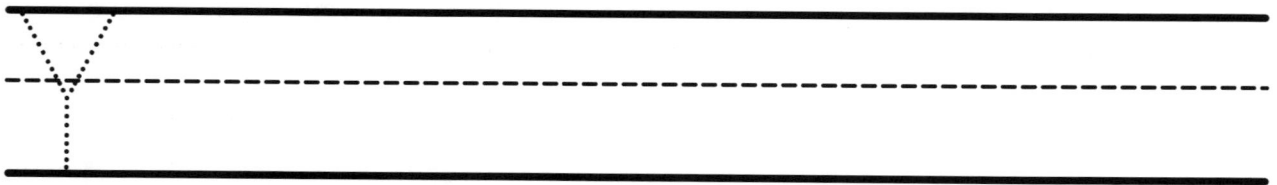

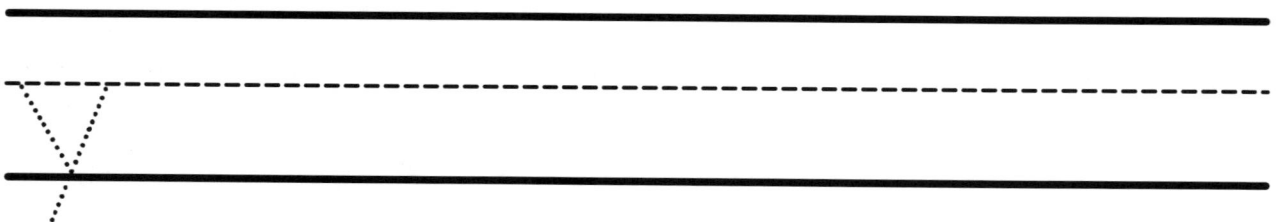

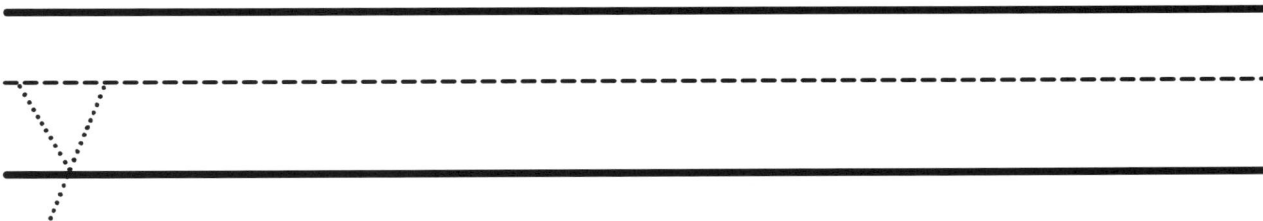

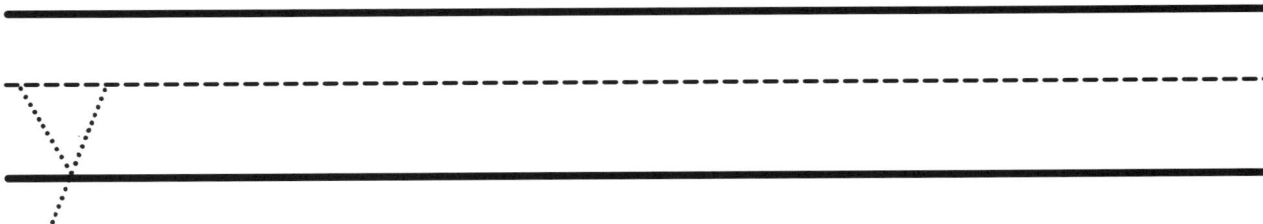

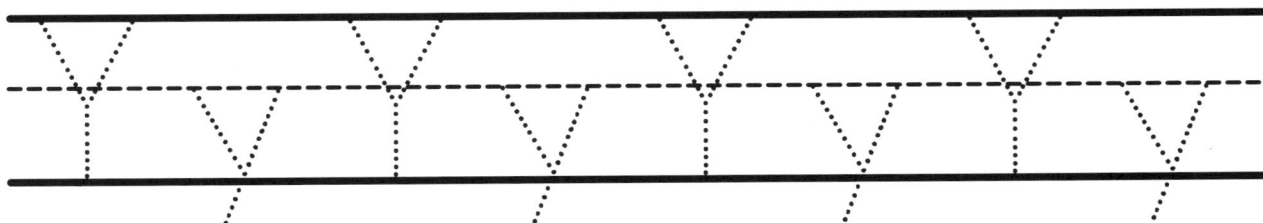

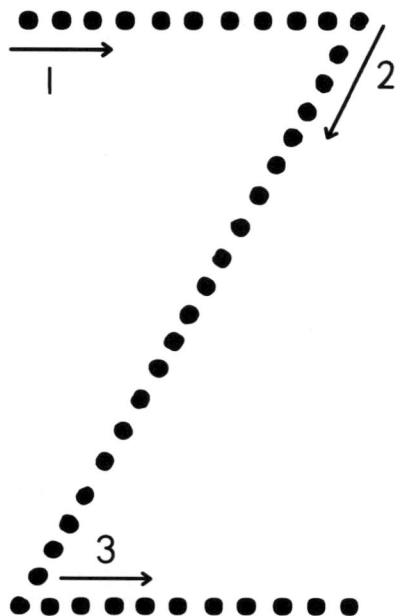

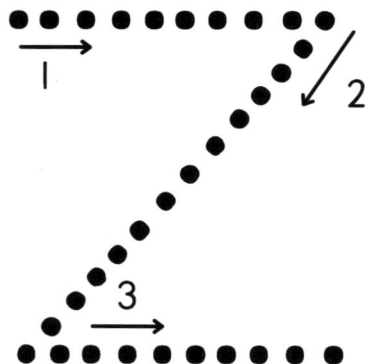

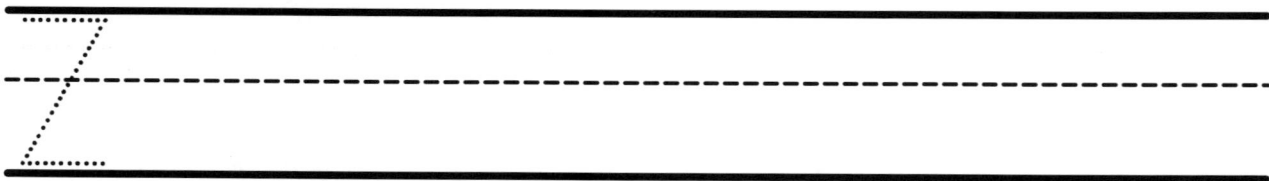

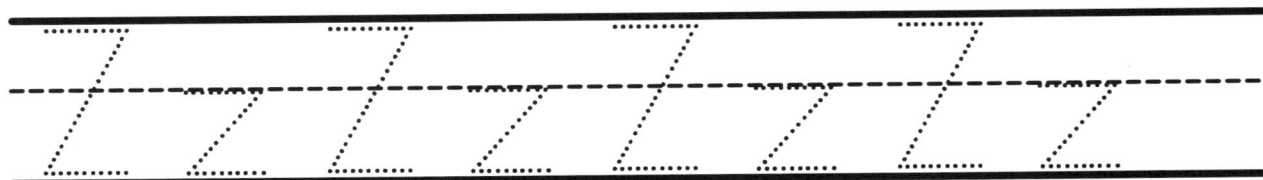

Numbers

One

Two

Three

Four

Five

Six

Seven

Eight

Nine

Ten

Eleven

Twelve

Thirteen

Fourteen

Fifteen

Sixteen

Seventeen

Eighteen

Nineteen

Twenty

Twenty One

Twenty Two

Twenty Three

Twenty Four

Twenty Five

Twenty Six

Twenty Seven

Twenty Eight

Twenty Nine

Thirty

Thirty One

Thirty Two

Thirty Three

Thirty Four

Thirty Five

Thirty Six

Thirty Seven

Thirty Eight

Thirty Nine

Forty

Forty One

Forty Two

Forty Three

Forty Four

Forty Five

Forty Six

Forty Seven

Forty Eight

Forty Nine

Fifty

Fifty One

Fifty Two

Fifty Three

Fifty Four

Fifty Five

Fifty Six

Fifty Seven

Fifty Eight

Fifty Nine

Sixty

Sixty One

Sixty Two

Sixty Three

Sixty Four

Sixty Five

Sixty Six

Sixty Seven

Sixty Eight

Sixty Nine

Seventy

Seventy One

Seventy Two

Seventy Three

Seventy Four

Seventy Five

Seventy Six

Seventy Seven

Seventy Eight

Seventy Nine

Eighty

Eighty One

Eighty Two

Eighty Three

Eighty Four

Eighty Five

Eighty Six

Eighty Seven

Eighty Eight

Eighty Nine

Ninety

Ninety One

Ninety Two

Ninety Three

Ninety Four

Ninety Five

Ninety-Six

Ninety Seven

Ninety Eight

Ninety Nine

Hundred

1 2 3 4 5 6

7 8 9 10 11

12 13 14 15 16

17 18 19 20 21

22 23 24 25

26 27 28 29

30 31 32 33

34 35 36 37

38 39 40 41

42 43 44 45

46 47 48 49

50 51 52 53

54 55 56 57

58 59 60 61

62 63 64 65

66 67 68 69

70 71 72 73

74 75 76 77

78 79 80 81

82 83 84 85

86 87 88 89

90 91 92 93

94 95 96 97

98 99 100

Sight Words

a an at are

a an at are

as at and all

as at and all

about after

about after

be by but been

be by but been

can could called

can could called

did down do

did down do

each from first

each from first

find for he his

find for he his

had how has

had how has

her have him

her have him

in I if into is

in I if into is

it its just know

it its just know

like long little

like long little

my made may

my made may

more many most

more many most

not no now

not no now

or one of out

or one of out

other over only

other over only

said she some

said she some

so see the to

so see the the to

they this there

they this there

them then these

them then these

two time than

two time than

that their up use

that their up use

very was with

very was with

what were when

what were when

we which will

we which will

would words where

would words where

water who way

water who way

Fruit's Name

Apple   Apple

Orange   Orange

Cherry   Cherry

Grape   Grape

Coconut Coconut

Mango Mango

Kiwi Kiwi

Plum Plum

Banana Banana

Peach   Peach

Papaya Papaya

Lemon Lemon

Apricot Apricot

Melon Melon

Simple Sentences

Get ready

Get ready

Get up

Get up

Give me

Give me

Go and play

Go and play

Go and study

Go and study

Hold it

Hold it

Hurry up

Hurry up

Keep quiet

Keep quiet

Look at me

Look at me

Listen to me

Listen to me

Have patience

Have patience

Hold my hand

Hold my hand

Made in the USA
Middletown, DE
14 November 2022